The Things That Make for PEACE

The Things That Make for PEACE

BIBLICAL MEDITATIONS

by Barbara A. Gerlach

BIP 90

The Pilgrim Press
New York

Library of Congress Cataloging in Publication Data

Gerlach, Barbara A., 1946–
    The things that make for peace.

    1. Peace (Theology)—Meditations.   2. Bible—
Meditations.   I. Title
BT736.4.G4   1983   261.8'73   83–4181
ISBN 0–8298–0664–4 (pbk.)

The Pilgrim Press, 132 West 31 Street, New York, New York 10001

To Jessica and Peter,
and all the world's children,
that they may know peace

Contents

List of Illustrations

Introduction

The biblical passages I have chosen to reflect on and write about are those that have touched me most deeply—words of peace that have comforted and confounded me, inspired and disturbed me, often both at the same time. The more I have searched the Bible and tried to enter the stories of people, similar and different from my own, the more my understanding of peace has been enlarged and clarified, grounded in life.

When I was first asked by *A.D.* magazine to write a yearlong series of Bible studies on peace, I hesitated. I am hardly a biblical scholar. Nor have I been particularly active in peace work. Others far more knowledgeable and involved than I are thinking about and working for peace.

I am an artist, not a writer. I was uncertain whether I could put my thoughts and struggles, hopes and fears about peace into words. I am a mother of small children. I was uncertain where I would find the time to read and reflect, to dig into myself and search the Bible, to collect my thoughts and shape the words that would bring me and others closer to the things that make for peace.

To be honest, many times I have despaired writing of peace—despaired because peace seems more hope than reality; despaired because the words of my faith and the facts of my life do not always fit together; despaired because no words adequately express the simplicity and complexity, the mystery and earthiness of the peace I have glimpsed in my own life and know more fully through the collected stories of the Bible.

As a writer, I have tried to be true both to what the Bible says and to the world I see. As an artist, I have found there are things I cannot say—the sighs too deep for words, the peace which passes understanding, the mystery of suffering that keeps us from peace and makes us seek it more fervently.

Most of the faces interspersed throughout the book were drawn before I began writing of peace. But as I wrote these faces haunted me. I realized I was wrestling with the same experience of suffering and hope as a writer and artist. My drawings and my writing belonged together as "companion meditations" on peace.

It has been said that we should read with the Bible in one hand, the newspaper in the other. My drawings are my attempt to see the struggle for peace in the world around me, to enter into the experience of the people who stare back at me from the newspaper. They are the contemporary faces of poverty and pain, violence and suffering, longing and hope to which our words and work for peace must speak.

The Things That Make for PEACE

❧ In the beginning, long before we claim or disclaim any religion, we are aware of being part of something greater than ourselves. In the beginning, long before we try to control the earth, we feel our kinship with it. ☙

In the Beginning

GENESIS 1:1—2:4

In the beginning God created the heavens and the earth. The earth was without form and void, and darkness was upon the face of the deep; and the Spirit of God was moving over the face of the waters. And God said, "Let there be light"; and there was light. And God saw that the light was good.

—Genesis 1:1-4

To go back to the beginning to discover where we come from is an urge as old as human life. Long before psychology led us back to infancy to find the roots of human personality, religion gave us stories to take us beyond our memories of childhood, beyond the history of our ancestors, back to the beginnings of life itself.

In the beginning, at God's first act of creation, is where the Bible—and the story of our spiritual roots—begins. And it is back to this beginning we turn seeking the peace we sense was ours and now seems lost.

For many of us, our first awareness of God and earliest intimations of peace are stirred by the beauty and harmony of creation. In the quiet of night and the breaking of day, in the bedrock of the mountains and the pulsing of the sea, in all that lives on the earth, we feel God living and moving. Behind and within creation we glimpse the hand of a creator—an animating spirit, a unifying presence, an underlying peace—so much greater than we.

This is the God in whose presence we stand in the opening lines of *Genesis*. Like our ancestors before us we are moved by the awesomeness of creation to ponder our origins and seek the One who made us.

Although the word peace is not used in the story, creation can be seen as the first act of peacemaking as God makes a world out of the primordial chaos and as a continuing source of revelation as we come to know God and glimpse God's peace through our experience of nature. What the story and our experience tell us is that the peace of creation is more than an inner state of well-being, more than concord with our fellow human beings, but an order and harmony that encompass the universe.

We witness this peace in the making in the Genesis story.

Not a show of strength in which God fights and subdues the forces of chaos, not a state of passivity in which God sits back and lets things be, peace comes in a dynamic act of creation as God's Spirit moves over the formless emptiness and calls a world out of deep darkness. Peace comes through work—God's work and ours. Insight and understanding, invention and art, intimacy and community are born as we move toward and work with the darkness and chaos that threaten our lives.

But the God of creation is not only Maker but Seer. Running through the story, following each day's work, is the refrain *and God saw that it was good*. Action is completed by contemplation, the work of creation by the rest of sabbath. And if this be so for God, how much greater our human need to rest and reflect, to move beyond the work of our hands and enjoy the goodness of creation.

After the heaven and earth, the day and night, the plants and animals, God creates human life. Distinct from the rest of creation by virtue of being created in God's image and given dominion over the earth, human beings enjoy a special relationship to God and a special responsibility for God's creation.

Threatened as we are by nuclear annihilation and the slow death of the earth from our misuse, we do not need the creation story to remind us how the fate of the earth lies in human hands. What we need to recover for our survival's sake is what it means to be *created in God's image*.

In the beginning, long before we claim or disclaim any religion, we are aware of being part of something greater than ourselves. In the beginning, long before we try to

control the earth, we feel our kinship with it. However vast
the difference between Creator and created, we experience a
very basic, even mystical, connection to God and all creation.

To go back to the beginning—carried by the measured
cadences of the creation story or stilled by the peace which
nature stirs—is to recover our deep relationship to both
Creator and creation. To go back to the beginning is to find
something of God, the Maker of peace and Seer of good, in
ourselves—in our creative urge and our longing for peace.
To go back to the beginning is to dwell with the earth in
creative harmony—God's relationship with us reflected in
our relationship with creation. To be created in the image
and likeness of God is to continue the work of God's
creation, exercising our dominion over the earth as
peacemakers and caretakers of all God made and saw
as very good.

✠ *After the fall the pursuit of peace is never simple.*
Good and evil dwell together; life is broken but not destroyed.
All creation groans in travail and yearns for peace. ✠

Their Eyes Were Opened

GENESIS 2:4—3:24

So when the woman saw that the tree was good for food, and that
it was a delight to the eyes, and that the tree was to be desired to
make one wise, she took of its fruit and ate; and she also gave
some to her husband, and he ate. Then the eyes of both were
opened, and they knew that they were naked.

—Genesis 3:6-7

My first years as a parish minister were the hardest of my
life. Visiting the sick, burying the dead, I was met by pain
and sorrow. Suffering was not an occasional intruder lurking
on life's edges, but an inescapable fact of existence striking
the rich as well as the poor, taking the young as well as the
old, shaking the peace of all of us.

We can all remember moments that marked our loss of
innocence, when our eyes were opened and we saw more
clearly the perplexing mix of good and bad which pervades
existence. To be human is to find this mix of good and evil
in ourselves, to wrestle with it as our moral dilemma, and
finally to acknowledge our conflict. No matter how hard we
try or how much we confess, we fail to do what we want to
do and we do the things that we hate (Romans 7:15).

This painful persistence of suffering and evil underlies
the story of the fall. The story begins with creation, viewed
not from the lofty heights of heaven (Genesis 1:1—2:4), but
from the intimacy of the earth (Genesis 2:4-25). God forms

human life out of the dust of the ground and plants a garden.

Life is good; the garden, a delight abounding in luscious fruit and animals of every kind. But more important is human companionship. God makes man and woman especially for each other. And with this exquisite sense of relatedness, as they recognize themselves as born of the same bone and sharing the same flesh, God's creation is complete.

If only the story ended here. But there is a tree in the middle of the garden, a tree of the knowledge of good and evil. It is from this tree and only this tree that God forbids the man and woman to eat (Genesis 2:16-17). As with all of us, the forbidden fruit is the most enticing.

Attention centers on the tree. Should they eat or should they not? Will they die or will they not? Is God's command intended to protect them from danger or keep them from the wisdom that could open their eyes and make them like God, knowing good and evil (Genesis 3:1-5)?

The lure of knowledge overcomes their fear of death. They eat and their eyes are opened. But instead of being like God, they know they are naked. Instead of being empowered by what they see, they are fearful and ashamed (Genesis 3:6-13).

The fall is the story of each one of us as we move from the innocent delight of childhood to self-knowledge and pain. Experience teaches us that life is not simply good, but full of conflict and ambiguity. Good and evil war within us, meet and mingle in all we do. No one is innocent; no one without shame.

In the plight of the first man and first woman we recognize our plight and the human condition. The earth that sustains us with its abundance is also hostile and destructive. The work that sometimes gives us pleasure is also tedious labor. Our relationships with one another, however well intended, are also flawed and broken (Genesis 3:14-19). The fall is comprehensive; all creation groans in travail (Romans 8:22).

It is not surprising that we all long to return to the garden, to the innocence of childhood and creation before the fall. But we are left with only a haunting memory of the peace we have lost. This memory can make us bitter, turning us away from life and locking us in a past we can never recapture. Or our yearning can grow into a vision of peace, making us strive for life's goodness.

Nor is it surprising that we are sometimes overwhelmed by the suffering and evil that are our lot. But we can dwell too long on the bad, blaming ourselves for our acts of wrongdoing, pitying ourselves for the pain that befalls us, rather than moving to the larger truth, the knowledge of *both* good and evil.

After the fall the mystery of suffering and evil remain, but life goes on. Even as the first couple are cursed to pain in childbirth, hard toil for their bread, and ultimately to death and the dust of the ground, the man names his wife Eve, mother of all living. Even as they are driven out of the garden, God makes garments to clothe and protect them (Genesis 3:19-24). Their peace is makeshift and imperfect, but human life and God's goodness survive.

After the fall the pursuit of peace is never simple. Good and evil dwell together; life is broken but not destroyed. All creation groans in travail and yearns for peace. But as we recognize the good and evil in ourselves and in others and as we see friend and enemy alike sharing the same hope and bearing the same pain, we find a new basis for human relatedness. The knowledge of good and evil that estranges us from one another can also lead to understanding and new bonds of peace.

Gerlach '80

✠ *Rather than eliminating life's contradictions, religion asks us to struggle with them, to ponder their meaning and live in their tension, until they lead us to deeper understanding and increase our capacity for life.* ✠

Peace and Righteousness Will Kiss

PSALM 85

Steadfast love and faithfulness will meet;
  righteousness and peace will kiss each other.
Faithfulness will spring up from the ground,
  and righteousness will look down from the sky.
                              —Psalm 85:10-11

"Speak the truth in love" (see Ephesians 4:15); "Be wise as serpents and innocent as doves [Matt. 10:16]." The language of religion is full of paradoxes. Rather than eliminating life's contradictions, religion asks us to struggle with them, to ponder their meaning and live in their tension, until they lead us to deeper understanding and increase our capacity for life.

The way of peace is strewn with tension and contradiction. In Psalm 85 the desire for peace and the demand for justice strain and struggle against each other until they finally meet and kiss.

Times are hard in Israel. The community is not prospering. The people, in desperation, cry out for the good life and the return of God's favor.

This psalm provides a good view of the Hebrew understanding of peace and the covenant relationship that lies at the center of the Hebrew religion. God and people, law and peace stand in reciprocal relationship. If the people are faithful to God and keep God's commandments, they enjoy God's favor and are blessed with peace. If they turn away from God and break the covenant, God turns away from them and breaks their peace. If the people return to God and mend their ways, God returns to them and their blessing is restored.

God makes the requirement for peace graphically clear. "If you walk in my statutes and observe my commandments and do them . . . I will give peace in the land, and you shall lie down, and none shall make you afraid [Lev. 26:3,6]." On the one side prosperity, security, and the community's well-being depend on keeping the covenant.

On the other side lies God's warning and judgment. "But if you will not hearken to me . . . but break my covenant, . . . I will appoint over you sudden terror . . . and cause life to pine away. And you shall sow your seed in vain, for your enemies shall eat it [Lev.26:14-16]." Land, cities, sanctuaries will be destroyed and the people scattered.

As they repeat the psalm the people recall God's covenantal promise to bless them. They remember former times when God forgave the people's sin and restored their good fortune (Psalm 85:1-3). They use the past to challenge God to put away anger and bless them again. "Show us thy steadfast love," they pray, "and grant us thy salvation [Ps. 85:5-7]."

Then the voice shifts. The people are called to hear God. But instead of listening, they anticipate the answer they want to hear. God will speak peace to the people and give them the prosperity for which they yearn (Psalm 85:8-9).

Finally God speaks. Peace is not so simple. There are obligations on both sides, and God reminds the people what is required of them. Their reciprocal responsibilities are paired in two couplets.

God will be steadfast in *love* only if the people are *faithful* to God. God's *peace* cannot be found apart from the people's *righteousness*. Only as the people are *faithful* to God and righteous in their relationships with their neighbors on earth will God be *righteous* to them and pour down blessing from heaven (Psalm 85:10-13).

The people are brought back to the commandments at

the center of the covenant. More than rules to be followed, the commandments have a much deeper significance for the Hebrew people. The law is God's revelation to them, their way of knowing God. As they reflect on the meaning of the law and struggle to live the commandments with their neighbors and even the strangers in their midst, they come to know God more deeply. God cannot be known apart from righteousness, apart from their right relationship with one another.

At the beginning of the psalm the people's longing for peace and God's demand for justice stand at odds. At the end the people's righteousness makes a way for God's peace (Psalm 85:13). At the heart of the psalm is the image of peace and righteousness kissing, as the people come to understand the intimate connection between peace and righteousness in their life together.

This psalm is not so much concerned with individual morality and salvation, but with the conduct and peace of a whole people and nation, the quality of their social relations, the justice of their dealings with one another and with other peoples and nations. Reading this psalm we, like the Hebrews who sang it long ago and the people who have repeated it through the ages, are challenged to reexamine our understanding of peace.

This psalm pushes us beyond any simple program for peace, even beyond our desire to beat all the weapons of war into plowshares. The demand for *righteous peace* forces us deeper—to right all the inequities and injustices that breed conflict and war, to challenge the prosperity that favors the rich and burdens the poor, devouring too much while millions go hungry.

Peace without righteousness is sentimentality that glosses over the violence of injustice, as the ease of a few rests on the affliction of many. Righteousness without peace is harsh legalism that breeds the violence of fanaticism, as one group forces its idea of right on another. True peace struggles with the tension between doing justice and making peace until the two are reconciled and peace and righteousness kiss.

✠ *As an artist, I have found there is a point where the line between myself and the people I draw breaks down, when their experience becomes part of me and touches mine. How shaken I was the first time this happened, while drawing a woman whose sons had been killed.* ✠

"Peace, Peace," When There Is No Peace

JEREMIAH 6:13-14

For from the least to the greatest of them,
   every one is greedy for unjust gain;
and from prophet to priest,
   every one deals falsely.
They have healed the wound of my people lightly,
   saying, "Peace, peace," when there is no peace.
                                   —Jeremiah 6:13-14

As an artist, I have found there is a point where the line between myself and the people I draw breaks down, when their experience becomes part of me and touches mine. How shaken I was the first time this happened, while drawing a woman whose sons had been killed. How great the sorrow she stirred in me, until I no longer knew what was hers and what was mine.

This is how Jeremiah speaks to me. His words are spoken at great personal cost. His identification with his people shakes him to the core and leaves him intolerant of the prophets who speak easily of peace, saying what the people want to hear and confusing God's peace with the preservation of their nation. For Jeremiah, peace entails terrible conflict—conflict with other nations that could not be avoided by false hope in God's intervention, conflict with his own people who rejected him and the judgment he spoke, conflict with the God who called him and his own desire to be left in peace.

The prophet and prophecy of *Jeremiah* explode with this

conflict. It is the end of the seventh century B.C., and power is shifting in the Mideast. The little nation of Judah is caught in the middle—too small to be a contender but trying to preserve its independence.

Within Jerusalem emotions run high. The sides are drawn, and the major actors are not the politicians, but the prophets. On one side are the temple prophets, saying, "Peace, peace," assuring the people that all will be well and promising God's protection. On the other side is the upstart Jeremiah, crying "Violence and destruction," warning of an end that is fast approaching, and voicing God's judgment. Everyone in Judah is guilty of false dealing. But worse than the rest, the priests and prophets are singled out for trying to heal deep wounds with light words of comfort.

It would be easy to cast Judah as the innocent victim, caught in an international situation beyond its control, no match for the powerful Babylon rising to the north. But Jeremiah holds his people responsible. They have brought destruction on themselves because they have failed to be true to God and just with their neighbors. Not peace, but sickness and wounds, is what Jeremiah sees. No balm can heal them, only the painful upheaval of God's judgment.

Such a message hardly qualifies Jeremiah—or his "dread warrior" God—as a pacifist. Yet peace is Jeremiah's passion; to destroy false peace and build true peace, his prophetic call (Jeremiah 1:9-10). To this end he opposes the false prophets and exposes their easy comfort as a lie. He smashes a clay pot to dramatize God's judgment, saying, likewise Judah will be broken beyond repair (Jeremiah 19:10-12).

But Jeremiah builds as well as destroys. When the end comes he writes to the defeated exiles in Babylon, encouraging them to build homes, plant gardens, bear children, and find their peace by seeking the peace of their captors.

Hardly easy words: to live in peace and pray for the welfare of their conquerors. But in their seventy-year captivity—stripped of the nation, land, and temple on which they thought their peace depended—their wounds will be healed, a new covenant forged, and a deeper understanding of peace written in their hearts (Jeremiah 29:5-14; 31:31-34).

What makes it possible for Jeremiah to see what others fail to see: the instability of power built on injustice, the deception of those who confuse God's peace with the security of their nation, the healing and reconciliation that can be born out of suffering?

Interspersed among his public pronouncements are Jeremiah's personal confessions, revealing his inner struggle to tell the truth even when it tears him apart and enrages his listeners. Far from the distance and objectivity we often seek, Jeremiah's understanding of peace is born from an excruciating empathy that takes him inside the God who calls him and the people to whom he must speak, making him feel both their experiences as his own and mediate between them.

It is presumptuous—even dangerous—to claim to speak with God's voice. But Jeremiah makes this claim. The lines blur between them. Is it God's anger or Jeremiah's, when the prophet cries: "I am full of the wrath of the Lord; I am weary of holding it in [Jer. 6:11]"? Is it God or Jeremiah weeping: "O that my head were waters, and my eyes a fountain of tears, that I might weep day and night for the slain . . . of my people [Jer. 9:1]"?

Jeremiah internalizes his peoples' experience as well. Their panic and grief are his. The commotion and dislocation of war go on inside his body: "My anguish, my anguish! I writhe in pain! . . . I cannot keep silent; for I hear the sound of the trumpet, the alarm of war [Jer. 4:19]." He is torn by their pain: "For the wound . . . of my people is my heart wounded [Jer. 8:21]."

In contrast to the false prophets who cover deep wounds with superficial words of comfort, true prophecy comes from and goes to the heart. Jeremiah is wounded to the heart by the suffering of his people. The exiles are stripped of everything, so they can return to God with all their heart. Even God's heart is revealed, painfully yearning for the scattered people, like a mother weeping for her lost children (Jeremiah 31:15-20).

There is no getting off lightly. Our wounds must be exposed for our sickness to be healed. The new covenant with God and true peace with our neighbors are born from the painful knowledge and empathetic meeting of our hearts.

⋈ *I have searched and drawn the faces of survivors of Nagasaki, Vietnam, South Africa, looking for the secret to their endurance.* ⋈

Good Tidings of Peace

ISAIAH 52—53

How beautiful upon the mountains
  are the feet of him who brings good tidings,
who publishes peace . . .
  who says to Zion, "Your God reigns."
  —Isaiah 52:7

For a long time I have been drawn by the stories of survivors. I have read the horrors recounted by Jews who survived the Nazi holocaust. As an artist, I have searched and drawn the faces of survivors of Nagasaki, Vietnam, South Africa, looking for the secret to their endurance.

It may be the curiosity of one whose life has been relatively privileged, wondering if I could survive such suffering. It may be the haunting awareness that such extremity, in the shape of nuclear disaster or unexpected personal tragedy, could suddenly strike any or all of us.

The Bible can be read as a book of survivors, of fall and flood, of captivity and crucifixion.

One such story is found in Isaiah 40—55. Authored by a prophet, himself a survivor of exile, and addressed to captives who had suffered defeat and deportation to a foreign land, "Second Isaiah" offers clues to what sustains a people ravaged by war and revives their hope of peace.

Here we find some of the most tender and exhilaratingly hopeful passages in the Bible: gentle words of comfort, visions of dark places made light and rough places smooth, and the voice of a herald bringing good tidings of peace. But hope is not the whole picture.

Two prophecies stand side by side. The first, read at Christmas in anticipation of the birth of Jesus, speaks of great joy—good news of deliverance from captivity (Isaiah 52:1-12). The second, read at Easter as foreshadowing the crucifixion, voices deep anguish—the sorrows of the suffering servant (Isaiah 52:13—53:12). But for the Jewish survivors of the sixth century B.C., these two prophecies were born from the same "furnace of affliction" (Isa. 48:10).

Hope did not come easy in Babylon. These were second- and third-generation exiles, worn down by long captivity, dulled to the "new thing" God was doing in their midst. We can feel the prophet's urgency as he cries, "Awake! Awake!" trying to stir their imagination, to rouse some hope in them.

Second Isaiah's hope is so rousing because it had to be. Only a great hope could overcome their debilitating fear.

But there is another side. In the face of such hope, what sense could they make of the suffering they had been through? If God was good and powerful enough to save them now, why had they suffered so and why would they suffer again?

Earlier prophets had answered by saying they had brought their suffering on themselves as punishment for their sins. But if this were so, what could account for their release? These were not the "true believers" or the "righteous remnant" who had earned their deliverance by great moral transformation or spiritual insight. These were a tired and dispirited people, oppressed as much by their own guilt and doubt as by the cruelty of their captors, suddenly free through no merit of their own.

Out of this contradiction of hope and suffering, guilt and forgiveness arose the image of the suffering servant. Something wonderful had happened. Yet in no way could they attribute their deliverance to themselves.

On one plane Cyrus of Persia had defeated the Babylonians and set the prisoners free. On another plane God was cutting a way through the desert, leading the exiles back home. On still another, a man of sorrows acquainted with the depth of their affliction had suffered for them, bearing their sin away.

Their hope incorporated the shadow side of their suffering. Suffering took on new meaning. No longer could it be seen only as punishment for sin, for they had experienced its redeeming power.

Nor could their faith be self-serving. They had been saved for a purpose: to be God's servants, a light to the nations, publishing peace and salvation to the ends of the earth.

Nor, after their defeat and deliverance at the hands of foreigners, could they imagine their peace apart from the peace of other nations. Their vision had been forced outward. God's reign, God's covenant of peace reached beyond Zion to all nations and all creation.

This is the peace proclaimed at Christmas as the angels say, "Be not afraid; for behold I bring you good news of a great joy which will come to all the people. . . . Glory to God in the highest, and on earth peace [Luke 2:10, 14]!"

Glimpsed in captivity, proclaimed to captives everywhere, this peace reaches wide enough to gather all people, deep enough to release the captive in each one of us. Our greatest hope and deepest suffering meet in the child who is both man of sorrows and prince of peace.

✣ It is when we are pushed to the edge of human possibility by our poverty or our grief, by our thirst for righteousness or our search for peace, by our suffering or our love that God meets us. ✣

Blessed Are
the Peacemakers

MATTHEW 5

You have heard that it was said, "You shall love your neighbor and hate your enemy." But I say to you, Love your enemies and pray for those who persecute you.

—Matthew 5:43-44

As a child, the Sermon on the Mount was my favorite part of the Bible. Something about Jesus' words spoke to my sense of what was right and called me as the way I wanted to live my life. To me, this was what religion was all about: a God who blessed the poor in spirit and pure in heart, people who turned the other cheek and walked the second mile.

Something has happened in the intervening years. Words that used to inspire my hope now sound harsh to my ears. I know myself and my world too well. I know the difficulty, the impossibility, even question the wisdom of living as Jesus taught.

I know my failures to love, my urge to retaliate, the anger and desire I harbor in my heart even when my actions do not betray me. Not much would be left if I cut off the eye or hand, the thought or feeling that caused me to sin.

Yet even as I come up against the impossibility of Jesus' words, something forces me to look again for what Jesus saw that I am missing.

One thing is certain: Jesus saw the world with different eyes. While others strained to see God and win God's blessing, Jesus declared: God's kingdom is here! God's blessing is now (Matthew 5:3-12)!

Not a far-off hope or a vague inner stirring, the words Jesus used are earthy and concrete. God's coming is as clear as a city on a hill that cannot be hid, the taste of salt on the tongue, the light of a lamp on a table (Matthew 5:13-15).

Even more striking is his claim that God comes through us. "You are the salt of the earth. You are the light of the world," Jesus exclaims. God enters the world and others see God through our good works (Matthew 5:16). The way Jesus sees it, human conditions affect God's coming. There is a vital connection between the quality of our lives, both inside and out, and our experience of God's blessing.

"Unless your righteousness exceeds that of the scribes and Pharisees, you will never enter the kingdom of heaven [Matt. 5:20]." This is a startling statement coming from one whom the scribes and Pharisees accused again and again of breaking the law.

Jesus makes his own position clear. He does not see himself as above the law or outside the tradition. He affirms God's commandments as the guide for our lives and the way to know God. He even goes so far as to say his life fulfills all the law and prophets promised (Matthew 5:17-20).

But more is required than following the law to the letter. Five times Jesus repeats, "You have heard it said . . . but I say to you." And each time he extends the law, making it radically new (Matthew 5:21-48).

Each time the "more" takes us to the edge of what is humanly possible. Not only are we not to kill, but we are not even to be angry. Not only are we to love our neighbor, but our enemy as well.

The old law had a certain balance: an eye for an eye, a tooth for a tooth. But the new law throws us off balance, calling us to turn the other cheek, walk the second mile, give more than we are asked. It expands infinitely beyond us until it ends on an absolutely impossible note: Be perfect as God is perfect (Matthew 5:48).

Only one other time does Jesus use the word perfect, as he answers the rich young man who asks what he must do to inherit eternal life. First, Jesus reviews the commandments, and then he adds, "If you would be perfect, go, sell what you possess and give to the poor . . . and come, follow me [Matt. 19:21]."

The full and perfect life is found when we move beyond the religious following of rules to the spontaneously generous act of love. God comes to us when we give ourselves to others.

In those moments of self-giving, inmost desire and outward deed overflow together. Our divided selves are made whole, and we experience God's blessing.

It is when we are pushed to the edge of human possibility by our poverty or our grief, by our thirst for righteousness or our search for peace, by our suffering or our love that God meets us. In these moments, which are our perfection and our peace, God comes to us as sure as the taste of salt on our tongues.

⊁ *The violence and suffering that accompany the pursuit of peace are felt most painfully in the conflict and division that tear homes and families apart.* ⊱

Not Peace
but a Sword

MATTHEW 10:34-39

Do not think that I have come to bring peace on earth; I have not
come to bring peace, but a sword. For I have come to set a man
against his father, and a daughter against her mother, and a
daughter-in-law against her mother-in-law.

—Matthew 10:34-35

I remember too well the tension in my family and so many
families during the war in Vietnam. One night in particular
stands out. I had stopped at my parents' home en route to a
peace demonstration. My parents, far more concerned about
my safety than my views on the war, urged me not to go.
Although I was quick to say I must, I spent the night torn
between honoring their wishes and following my conscience,
sobered by the distance and division that had come between
us. The next morning I continued on my way, less easy than
when I started. In that sleepless night I glimpsed the conflict
and contradiction that shadow the pursuit of peace.

Painful moments, uneasy decisions like this one come to
mind as I try to understand Jesus' startling statement: "I
have not come to bring peace, but a sword." Three things
strike me about his disturbing words.

First, they are terrifying. These are not his enemies Jesus
is warning, but his dearest friends and followers he is
entrusting with his ministry and sending out with a message
of peace. But the terrible fact remains. Peace does not come

without conflict. The peacemakers will be persecuted. The bearers of love will be hated and maligned (Matthew 10:1-25).

Second, they are true. True to the baiting and beating and torturous death that Jesus suffered. True to the persecution the disciples received at the hands of religious and political authorities. True to the fate of contemporary peacemakers: Mahatma Gandhi, Martin Luther King Jr., Anwar es-Sadat—all killed by those who opposed their message of peace and feared the new order they were creating.

Third, they strike too close to home. Father is set against son, mother against daughter, mother-in-law against daughter-in-law. The violence and suffering that accompany the pursuit of peace are felt most painfully in the conflict and division that tear homes and families apart (Matthew 10:34-36).

God calls, and twelve-year-old Jesus stays behind to talk to the teachers in the temple, rather than obediently following his parents home (Luke 2:41-51). Jesus calls, and James and John leave their father and their fishing nets behind to follow him (Matthew 4:21-22); women leave their homes and follow too (Matthew 27:55).

It is not that Jesus takes lightly the bonds of love and constancy that hold families together. On other occasions he urges his listeners to honor their parents (Matthew 15:4-9), to be faithful in marriage (Matthew 19:3-9), to learn from their children (Matthew 18:1-6).

But for Jesus there is a greater and more urgent claim on life than devotion to family. God comes first. To love God means conflict with all our other loves—love of family, love of peace, love of life itself.

Jesus offers no escape from the conflict. He does not say, leave your family and be free of the conflict, only that we are to love him more than our fathers or mothers, sons or daughters (Matthew 10:37). Nor does he say that by loving God all the conflicting claims of work and family, self and others will be resolved. Jesus is clear about the cost. To put God first means conflict—conflict with family and pain for those we love the most.

Jesus knew this conflict from experience. His sense of

himself as God's son kept him from being the son his parents wanted. He saw the pain reflected in his mother's eyes as she pondered the meaning of his birth, worried over him as a child, watched his slow death on a cross—his life, their life as a family ended before its time.

In our own less dramatic ways we know the conflict too. Some time or another we have felt like strangers in our own homes, separated by longings we cannot express, convictions we cannot explain, commitments we cannot give up. We have experienced our families as our enemies—our devotion and duty to them, our fear of losing their love or approval holding us back from following some deeper claim on our lives.

"Who is my mother, and who are my brothers?" Jesus asked, when told his family had come to see him. Stretching out his hands toward his disciples he answered, "Here are my mother and my brothers!" Whoever does the will of God is his brother, and his sister, and his mother (Matthew 12:48-50).

Jesus comes and disturbs the little peace we have. He calls us away from our too-narrow attachments to our own families. He extends us beyond ourselves, beyond our parents and children to a new sense of family in which all people are our brothers and sisters, mothers and fathers, sons and daughters.

It is easy to say these words but hard to be this family. The way of peace leads through conflict and contradiction, through suffering and death. To walk this way is never to speak easily of peace again.

✣ *At the heart of the resurrection lies the mystery of suffering. Suffering can destroy or create, move us to love or move us to hate.* ✣

The Things That Make for Peace

LUKE 19:28-42

And when he drew near and saw the city he wept over it, saying,
"Would that even today you knew the things that make for peace!
But now they are hid from your eyes."

—Luke 19:41-42

"Peace on earth!" sang the angels at Jesus' birth. "Peace
in heaven!" shouted the disciples as he journeyed toward
Jerusalem and a week that would end on a cross.

What is it about this man—born in a stable, riding to
death on a donkey—that stirs our praise and makes us
believe in peace again? "Peace" we sing with the angels.
"Peace" we shout with the crowd. Even the stones seem to
cry out: "Blessed be the King who comes in the name of the
Lord! Peace in heaven and glory in the highest [Luke 19:38]!"

The scene shifts. The singing and shouting give way to
sorrow; the public praise, to private pain. The man we call
"Blessed" separates himself from the crowd and stands
alone, weeping over the city he is about to enter.

He senses the suffering that awaits him, the cost of the
peace we so eagerly proclaim. He answers our joy with a sad
foreboding: "Would that even today you knew the things
that make for peace! But now they are hid from your eyes
[Luke 19:41-42]."

His suffering is not hidden long. Jesus enters the city

and goes to the temple to preach. His words arouse the crowd and incense the authorities.

Betrayed by one of his own disciples, he does not resist arrest or the cruelty of his captors. Made a public spectacle, he is mocked, beaten, and nailed to a cross to die. Every twist of pain, every cry of anguish is jeered as evidence of his weakness and proof of his defeat.

When his passion for peace is over, violence has won. Jesus is dead; his following is broken.

But on the third day strange things begin to happen.

Women go to the tomb with spices for the dead man's body. They find the stone rolled away and the body gone.

Two men are walking to a nearby town, talking intently. Jesus joins their conversation and later eats with them. Not until he is breaking bread do they recognize him, and he vanishes from their sight.

Back in Jerusalem, people are gathering and recounting the strange events of the day. Suddenly, Jesus stands among them. Some fear he is a spirit until he invites them to touch his body and look at his hands and feet.

Each time his followers *see* something that convinces them that Jesus is alive, they *hear* something that helps them *understand* his suffering and death.

Remember what Jesus told you, *believe* what the prophets have spoken, *understand* what is written in the scriptures— the women at the tomb, the travelers on the road, the followers in Jerusalem are told in turn. And each time their memories stir, their hearts burn with essentially the same words: *The Christ must suffer and on the third day rise* (Luke 24:5-7, 24-26, 44-47).

At the heart of the resurrection lies the mystery of suffering. Suffering can destroy or create, move us to love or move us to hate.

We do not need the cross to show us the destructive power of suffering, so great that even the Christ dies, even God weeps. We are all people of sorrow, acquainted with pain and grief, hatred and violence; all victims of the inescapable darkness of death.

What we do not expect to find on Easter, and in all the darkest moments of our lives, is the power of suffering to save, to move us through death to life, through pain to joy, through violence to love. "Love bears all things . . . endures all things" is the way the apostle Paul describes the persistent movement of the crucifixion and resurrection through the anguish of suffering and death to the ultimate triumph of love and life (1 Corinthians 13:7).

We suffer not only because evil is inescapable and the power of darkness great. We suffer because to bear and share the suffering of others is the ultimate act of love.

The peace of Christmas is easier to sing—the birth of a baby still untouched by sorrow. The peace of Palm Sunday is easier to praise—the mighty works of a humble king still unmarked by defeat. But the peace of Easter—so riddled by suffering we can hardly believe it—is the peace that triumphs in our darkest hours.

Would that you knew the things that make for peace. The words come back to us. The weeping becomes more clear. The cross is more than senseless violence, but the suffering that makes for peace.

⚜ The Spirit is the indwelling presence who comes to help us in our moments of greatest need, voicing our sighs too deep for words, praying for us when we cannot speak. ⚜

Peace I Leave with You

JOHN 14:25-27

These things I have spoken to you, while I am still with you. But the Counselor, the Holy Spirit . . . will teach you all things, and bring to your remembrance all that I have said to you. Peace I leave with you; my peace I give to you; not as the world gives do I give to you. Let not your hearts be troubled, neither let them be afraid.

—John 14:25-27

Peace I leave with you—so Jesus bids farewell to his disciples and prepares them for his death, promising his peace even as he leaves them. How often we have heard these words repeated at times of death and felt their power to comfort us. In the final and most wrenching of separations we are assured that all is not lost.

My peace I give to you. Even as the words are comforting, they are mystifying. What is clear to Jesus is confusing to us. Peace is promised, but we are not sure what it will look like or how to obtain it. Like the disciples, we are left with more questions than answers. We want the whole picture, but we see dimly, partially, intermittently. So much remains unknown.

Yet it is as if Jesus anticipated our problem: the limits of what he could tell us and we can understand; the limits of answers given on the eve of his death to satisfy the questions of all time; the limits of any and all words to carry the inexpressible mystery of God.

These things I have spoken to you, while I am still with you. But the Counselor, the Holy Spirit . . . will teach you all things. Jesus does not tell us everything; he does not claim to be THE ANSWER. What he offers is a Spirit, intimately involved in our lives, teaching us as we go. If Jesus is the light of the world, God's word made flesh to show us how to live more fully and truly, then the Spirit is the light that keeps breaking on our lives, God's voice that keeps speaking in and through us.

The descriptions of how the Spirit helps us are some of the most reassuring and empowering in the Bible. The Spirit is the indwelling presence who comes to help us in our moments of greatest need, voicing our sighs too deep for words, praying for us when we cannot speak (Romans 8:26-27). The Spirit is the unifying force who brings us together, giving us a common language so people of different backgrounds, circumstances, and perspectives can understand one another (Acts 2:1-13). The Spirit is the power of prophecy that does not stop with Jesus but keeps filling us—men and women, young and old, menservants and maidservants—with the power to see visions and dream dreams (Acts 2:14-22).

The Counselor . . . will bring to your remembrance all that I have said to you. The Spirit is also our connection to the past and our link to the future, bringing to mind and to life the words that Jesus spoke long ago, making old stories of peace echo as our own. Through the living memory that the Spirit quickens in each succeeding generation, we are joined in our search for peace with people through time.

My peace I give to you; not as the world gives do I give to you. For many of us, the peace that comes with the Spirit is the most real and immediate experience of God in our lives, but it is also the most elusive. We cannot see the Spirit, but we feel it dwelling in us and among us, drawing us together and drawing us toward God. We recognize the Spirit in the works of love that issue from it.

If we love him, Jesus says, if we love one another as he loved us, then God will give us another Counselor to be with us forever, a Spirit of truth, who will dwell with us and in us (John 13:34; 14:15-17). The God who created us and our world, Jesus who came to us as our friend on earth, the Spirit of truth who makes its home with us forever—they are one and continuous, all joined and revealed in the act of love. When we love one another the Spirit is known to us and shown to others.

Let not your hearts be troubled. Peace can have many meanings: absence of war, resolution of conflict, release from suffering. It can be an inner state of quiet, like peace of mind or heart. It can be an external condition of well-being, like the peace and welfare of a community. But the peace Jesus promises in the Gospel of John is slightly different.

Our peace comes from a sense of *presence*, an indwelling Spirit who comforts and strengthens us in every moment and circumstance and condition of our lives. Our peace comes from the assurance of *knowledge*, a Spirit of truth who helps us remember and guides us when we are lost and shows us the way. Our peace comes from the power of *love*, a unifying Spirit who closes the distance and differences that separate us from God and from one another, bringing us together and making us one.

Neither let them be afraid. The Spirit tells the truth and does not gloss over the harsh reality of our lives—inner torment, broken relationships, social upheaval, war and fear of war. The truth is frightening. Peace is promised and Jesus is crucified. Peace is promised and the disciples are not spared suffering. Peace is promised and violence is still in our streets, our homes, and our hearts.

The peace Jesus gives is not the peace the world gives, not the peace we expect. Our conflicts are not eliminated; our suffering is not taken away. But we are not left bereft. In the most wrenching moments of our lives we find help and peace. We are not afraid because a Spirit, who knows the truth and loves the world, gives us what is needed.

🗤 My hungry baby, the faces of starving children call me back to the most basic human need, to a body warmed and filled. 🗤

Go in Peace, Be Warmed and Filled

JAMES 2:14-17

If a brother or sister is ill-clad and in lack of daily food, and one of you says to them, "Go in peace, be warmed and filled," without giving them the things needed for the body, what does it profit? So faith, by itself, if it has no works, is dead.

—James 2:15-17

My husband and I adopted our first child, a little girl from Colombia, at a time when the newspapers were filled with stories of starvation. Experiencing for myself the fury of a hungry baby and the pleasure of feeding her, realizing how much the peace of our child and our home depended on her full belly made those pictures of mothers with their starving children call out to me. Suddenly, I knew how terrible it would be to have no food to answer a baby's cry, to hear the wailing grow louder and louder, and even worse to feel that little body grow weaker and weaker in my arms.

This is the picture I see when *James* challenges the faith that promises peace but fails to feed the hungry and clothe the ill-clad. My hungry baby, the faces of starving children call me back to the most basic human need, to a body warmed and filled.

What does it mean to talk of peace? What is required when we offer that hope to another? These are the questions the unknown writer of the letter of *James* answers very simply: Faith without works is dead.

His was a practical faith, as concerned with what we do as what we believe. Work matters. Faith alone cannot save us; words alone cannot fill us. When it comes to peace, James is clear: "Be doers of the word [James 1:22]."

Work is what makes our words clear. To say "I love my daughter" is empty without the daily and sometimes tedious tending of her body. To say "Go in peace" is meaningless unless our words of blessing are followed by our work for peace.

Every one of us hopes and dreams of peace. Every religion, every political movement offers its vision, its version of what that peace will be. But the peace of God, made flesh in the life of Jesus, is a particular kind of peace: peace for the poor, the sick, the outcast; peace for those in deepest need.

When Jesus said he came to preach good news to the poor, he meant it (Luke 4:18). He fed those hungering for food and for righteousness. He healed the sick of their bodily afflictions and their inner torments. He welcomed our whole being, spiritual longing and physical need. He preached with words that lived in deeds.

Be doers of the word, writes James, and you will be blessed in your doing (James 1:25). It is a curious turn of phrase. So often our work focuses on the benefit accrued to the receiver, but James reminds us of the blessing that comes to the giver as well.

Surrounded as we are by overwhelming human need, the emphasis on work sounds obvious, tedious, even hopeless—hardly a source of blessing! No matter how hard we try, no matter how much we do, our work alone cannot bring peace to the world. Our hope does not lie in the strength of our accomplishments, which are small compared to the great need that inspires them.

We are blessed in our doing because God blesses our deed. We are blessed as we work because the place of meeting, the moment of communion, between giver and receiver, is the place, the moment, of God's revelation and grace.

This is the mystery of our faith, the unexpected surprise. As we feed the hungry, clothe the naked, welcome the stranger, visit the sick or the prisoner, Jesus comes to us and says, as you have done it to these, my sisters and brothers, you have fed and clothed, welcomed and visited me (Matthew 25:31-46).

Think of a time when you have reached out to someone in need and found yourself beyond your knowledge of what to do, beyond your capacity to help, yet filled with a sense of "something" working in and through you. God present in your presence, God speaking through you.

This is the blessing that comes to the faithful worker. God comes to us and works through us. These are some of the most peace-filled moments of our lives, when our faltering efforts are infused and magnified by the blessing of God.

✻ *The survival of our planet depends on breaking down the dividing walls of nation and class, race and sex, religion and political ideology . . . seeing ourselves, above all our other identities, as one body and members one of another.* ✻

Breaking Down the Dividing Wall

EPHESIANS 2:11-22

For he is our peace, who has made us both one, and has broken down the dividing wall of hostility.

—Ephesians 2:14

"Do you accept Jesus Christ as your personal savior?" is a question that has always troubled me. It is not that the question puts me on the spot to declare where I stand in relation to Jesus. Rather, it strikes me as the wrong question, based on too narrow a view of peace and salvation.

Confessing Jesus as personal savior has always sounded to me like claiming Christ's peace as if it were a personal possession, the product of a private transaction between Jesus and me. By focusing on the individual person, it separates my peace from the peace, or misfortune, of other people.

Paul offers another view of Christ's peace in his letter to the Ephesians. Here the focus is not on personal salvation, but on how we have been made *alive together* (Ephesians 2:5).

According to Paul, the purpose of God's salvation, set forth in the life and teachings of Jesus, is to unite all things in heaven and earth (Ephesians 1:10). More than a feeling of oneness with God, more than a conviction that deep down we are all one with another, Christ's peace actually changes the relationship between people and brings us together.

Paul's example of Christ's unifying peace is drawn from an experience he and the Ephesians share.

He was a Jew. They were gentiles. The hostility between them was deep and long standing. It was not hard for those gentile converts to Christianity to remember how they had been treated by Jews like Paul, the names they had been called, the walls erected by Jewish law that kept them apart, the marks of circumcision and uncircumcision that signed and sealed their differences (Ephesians 2:11-12).

But something had happened to change all this. An experience of peace had brought the hostility to an end (Ephesians 2:13-17).

Paul recounts the story of this peace from his Jewish perspective. It is the story of Jesus Christ, the long-awaited Messiah, but with an unexpected twist. Ringing through Paul's conversion to Christianity and his call to preach to the gentiles was the startling realization that Jesus had come not only to save the Jews, but the rest of the world as well.

It must have been a remarkable time, those early years of Christianity, as a new mix of people came together for the first time. Jews and gentiles worked and worshiped together, ate at the same table, met in each other's homes, no longer strangers and aliens but fellow citizens and members of the same household of God (Ephesians 2:18-19).

When Paul wrote that Christ had broken down the dividing wall of hostility, creating one new person where there had been two, he was describing this newfound community. The peace Jesus announced during his life was being fleshed out by new converts to Christianity who had neither seen Jesus nor witnessed his resurrection, but who experienced him alive in their midst, knitting and joining them together.

Their community was the dynamic center of their faith. God's dwelling was not a temple made of stone, not even the souls of individual believers, but a living body of people joined and growing together (Ephesians 2:20-22).

Nor was the dwelling finished. The prophets and apostles were the foundation; Jesus, its cornerstone. But each and every person had to be built lovingly and patiently into it for God's dwelling to be complete.

Nor was the building easy. Paul's letters are filled with

the difficulties encountered by people who stood on opposite sides of the dividing wall—Jew and gentile, slave and free, male and female—as they struggled in truth and in love to shape their spirit of unity into lasting bonds of peace.

To become one was not to become the same. Jews did not become gentiles nor gentiles Jews, but together they both became something new. The task was not to make people to fit an existing structure, walling them in or walling them out, but to create a living structure, one body of people joined and growing together, to be God's dwelling and body on earth.

More than an end of conflict, more than peaceful coexistence, these early Christians found in their coming together a larger identity and deeper bond that broke through the dividing walls and turned hostility into community. They experienced themselves more alive together than they had been apart.

In a perverse way the desperation of our world forces us to a similar realization. The threat of nuclear annihilation, the slow death of our earth from human misuse, the crisis of exploding population and shrinking resources show us that we live or die together.

The survival of our planet depends on breaking down the dividing walls of nation and class, race and sex, religion and political ideology. The fate of future generations depends on our seeing ourselves, above all our other identities, as one body and members one of another.

❧ *Between what we ask for and what we receive lies an unfathomable mystery. We are answered, not with the simple fulfillment of our wishes, but with a power and presence so much greater than we, with the gracious peace of God.* ❧

The Peace Which Passes All Understanding

PHILIPPIANS 4:4-7

Rejoice in the Lord always; again I will say, Rejoice. Let
all . . . know your forbearance. The Lord is at hand. Have no
anxiety about anything, but in everything by prayer and
supplication with thanksgiving let your requests be made known to
God. And the peace of God, which passes all understanding, will
keep your hearts and your minds in Christ Jesus.

—Philippians 4:4-7

After the funeral of Robert Moss, president of the United
Church of Christ, several of us were sharing our recollections
of Bob, as we often do when someone we love has died. Our
stories spanned his lifetime, but eventually focused on the
remarkable things Bob had done during the last few weeks
of his life, acts that witnessed to his faith, showed his love,
and drew us together.

We had all prayed for the miracle that would stop the
cancer. The miracle had not come, the cancer had won. Yet
the memories shared round that room told another story.
There was loss and uncertainty, to be sure. But a lively sense
of Bob and the faith that compelled and comforted him kept
breaking through our sorrow.

Finally, someone found words to express how we were

strengthened by Bob's death as well as bereaved. "There is a grace that comes," he said, "when healing isn't possible."

A grace that comes when healing is not possible. A peace which passes all understanding. It is not that the struggle for healing and understanding is useless. Certainly loving God with heart, mind, soul, and strength means bringing all we are—our best thoughts and deepest feelings, our inarticulate longing, and the force of our actions—to pursue God's peace. But there is a place where words fail and our best efforts are not enough and the peace that comes is beyond our understanding.

Perhaps all experiences of peace—from the simplest intimacy between two people to the most complicated negotiations between warring nations—have some element we cannot account for. But at certain moments we are more deeply aware, more desperately in need of the peace that is God's, and not our own making.

Think of the incurable disease that takes the life of someone we love, the death that marks our human separation; the war and injustice that erupt in ever more virulent forms, haunting us generation after generation; the blind and unyielding parts of ourselves that resist change, no matter what we try. How do we survive the violent and senseless forces of evil, the dark and turbulent nights of our souls, without the peace of God? And more than survive, how do we come through with some joy remaining?

I confess what anyone who looks at the faces I draw can see. I have a better eye for suffering, for the mixing of joy and sorrow, than I do for the wholehearted rejoicing that Paul emphatically claims is ours.

I have little patience for the blind joy of those who fail to see the sufferings of the world. I am skeptical of those whose joy seems forced, happy no matter what befalls them. But there is another joy—deeper than the good times and bad times life metes out, stronger than our best attempts and sorest failings—a joy that lifts us when we cannot lift ourselves, a peace that grasps us and returns us renewed.

This is the joy Paul proclaims, as he writes to the Philippians from prison. *Rejoice in the Lord,* for our deepest joy lies not in our circumstances, but in God. *Let all . . . know your forbearance.* To know the joy that comes from God is not to be carried away in blissful happiness, but to be strengthened and deepened in our love for the world.

The Lord is at hand. Have no anxiety about anything, but in everything by prayer . . . let your requests be made known. We have nothing to fear for God is with us. Desperate cries, heartfelt thanks—nothing is too large or small to be taken and to take us to God.

And the peace of God, which passes all understanding, will keep your hearts and your minds in Christ Jesus. Between what we ask for and what we receive lies an unfathomable mystery. We are answered, not with the simple fulfillment of our wishes, but with a power and presence so much greater than we, with the gracious peace of God.

Paul closes his letter from prison with a personal confession of how God through Jesus Christ has strengthened him: "For I have learned, in whatever state I am, to be content. I know how to be abased, and I know how to abound; in any and all circumstances I have learned the secret of facing plenty and hunger, abundance and want [Phil. 4:11-12]." This is the peace which passes all understanding, the grace that comes when healing is not possible.

DATE DUE

8/17/87		
3/4/88		
MAY 1 4 1989		
DEC 0 5 1989		
NOV 0 2 1990		
10-27-90		
MAR 2 1 1995		
APR 0 1 1996		
WITHDRAWN		
GAYLORD		PRINTED IN U.S.A.